Lancaster County

Churches

in the

Revolutionary War Era

Lancaster County

Churches

in the

Revolutionary War Era

Lancaster

A BICENTENNIAL BOOK

1976

Lancaster County Churches in the Revolutionary War Era
ISBN 0-915010-11-9

Copyright © 1976 by Lancaster County Historical Society

Printed in the United States of America

Library of Congress Catalog Card No. 76-21210

A BICENTENNIAL BOOK *published by*
LANCASTER COUNTY BICENTENNIAL COMMITTEE, INC.
Co-published and distributed by
Sutter House
Box 146, Lititz, Pa. 17543

Contents

Introduction

MATTHEW W. HARRISON, JR.

THE HISTORY OF EARLY CHURCH LIFE in Lancaster County is the story of realized hopes for freedom of worship among people fleeing religious persecution in Europe.

It is the story of hardy settlers in the wilderness who built places to pray while they built shelter for their families.

It is the story of totally committed men such as Martin Boehm, an early leader in the Mennonite, Brethren in Christ and United Methodist Churches; Francis Asbury, Philip William Otterbein and Henry Melchior Muhlenberg, pre-eminent Colonial American churchmen who played active roles in Lancaster County church activities; Jacob Albright, the "honest tile maker" who founded a denomination here before he died at age 49; and Christian Newcomer, born a Mennonite and later a bishop in the United Brethren (now United Methodist) Church, who covered a "circuit" extending from Philadelphia to Indiana, and from Virginia to Canada, and who crossed the Allegheny Mountains a total of forty-eight times—almost a life's work in itself considering the rigors of frontier travel two centuries ago.

It is the story of denominations, some of which, notably the Evangelical Congregational Church and the Brethren in Christ Church, were founded in Lancaster County, while others, transplanted from Europe, took root and flourished here.

This brief volume is intended to chronicle Lancaster County's church history only through the eighteenth century. Its main purpose is to describe the work of the pioneer churchmen and laymen who started and built our religious institutions during the Colonial period, the Revolutionary War and the early days of our Republic.

These early settlers, as Ralph Waldo Emerson said of Michaelangelo, "builded better than they knew." More than eighty Lancaster County churches founded prior to 1800 are still active today. This includes the county's oldest church, the Willow Street Mennonite Congregation, founded in 1710.

These Colonial church histories are, for the most part, drawn from more extensive papers prepared by knowledgeable members of the denominations represented herein. The authors deserve the gratitude of everyone who shares the belief that our religious heritage, as well as our political and governmental wellsprings, is worth exploring in this Bicentenial year.

MATTHEW W. HARRISON, JR., EDITOR

The Mennonites & Amish

MARTIN E. RESSLER

THE MENNONITES are the oldest religious body or sect to be permanently established in Lancaster County. They also formed the first white settlement in the area, located directly south and east of present-day Lancaster City.

A total of thirty-one Mennonite congregations established in Lancaster County during the eighteenth century are still active today. Of these, twenty-six predate the signing of the Declaration of Independence, and one— the Willow Street Congregation—dates back to 1710.

The Mennonite Church originated in Zurich, Switzerland, in the year 1525. Certain followers of Ulrich Zwingli were unable to accept the course which he and Martin Luther had taken in setting up a Protestant state church system. Mennonites wanted the church to be composed only of believers—men and women who had had an experience with God and who had committed their lives in unreserved obedience to His word.

One of the basic causes of Mennonite conflict with the state churches was infant baptism. Anabaptists contended that the New Testament Church was constituted of persons who knowingly chose to accept Jesus Christ as their Lord and Savior and acknowledged this through receiving the rite of baptism.

The founders of this new movement were not initially known by the name Mennonite. At first they were simply

1

known as "Brethren." As this group continued to grow in Europe, the founding group in Switzerland became known as the "Swiss Brethren." The enemies of the Brethren called them Anabaptists, which literally means rebaptizers. This name was given them because they insisted that all believers must be rebaptized if they had been baptized only as infants.

The three men who started this movement were Conrad Grebel, Felix Manz and George Blaurock. All three were very capable leaders; however, they did not have long to live. As the church grew, so did persecution. New congregations began to form in other areas. Wherever these congregations started, government authorities tried in vain to stop them. Members were imprisoned, cruelly tortured and fined, but to no avail. Finally in 1527, authorities imposed the death penalty. The first one of these believers to give his life for his faith was Felix Manz. He was drowned in the Limmat River, Switzerland, on January 5, 1527. Conrad Grebel had died a few months earlier as a result of the plague. George Blaurock was burned at the stake at Clausen on September 6, 1529.

The grim reality that the founding leaders were now removed from their midst did not, however, destroy the zeal of the group. Anabaptists continued to spread across Germany toward Holland and continued to teach as they went. It appears that the first of these believers came to northwest Germany and Holland in 1530. They continued to gain converts as they crossed the Netherlands.

In 1536 the Anabaptists won to their cause a very able Catholic priest, Menno Simons. Shortly after his baptism, Simons was persuaded to accept ordination as an elder or bishop and soon became the outstanding leader of the group. Gradually thereafter these Anabaptists began to be known as "Menists," "Mennonists," and later as "Mennonites." Severe perseuction continued against the Swiss Brethren as they gradually spread into various parts of Germany and Switzerland. The chief place of refuge in the earlier years of this oppression was in the Palatinate, just north of Alsace and on both sides of the Rhine. Even here there were strict limitations. Worship was permitted in groups of not more than twenty people. No meetinghouses were to be built, no baptisms could be performed, no rights of citizenship could be granted, and annual protection money had to be paid.

When William Penn, a Quaker, received a grant of land in America in 1681 from the King of England as payment for a debt owed to his father, he opened this territory as a haven to the religiously persecuted peoples of Europe. They welcomed this invitation, and within the next several decades they began to arrive in large numbers. Among the first of these immigrants were a group of Mennonites who in 1683 settled at Germantown near the "City of Brotherly Love." This became the first permanent Mennonite settlement in America.

In 1710 a much larger Mennonite community, later referred to as the Pequea settlement, marked the beginning of Lancaster County. Early records show that the families who first came here were so well pleased with the community that they wanted to make provision for other families to join them. Within the first year they made application to purchase ten thousand acres of land adjacent to their settlement. Part of this territory was patented to them on September 10, 1710.

The most treasured landmark of this first settlement is

the Herr House, situated a short distance east of the village of Willow Street. On the stone lintel above the door is cut this lettering: 17 * CHHR * 19, which means that this house was built by Christian Herr in the year 1719. Christian was the son of the older Hans Herr, who was among the first group to arrive. This old restored house stands as a memorial to these early pioneers.

While most of the early Mennonites continued as farmers, there were always those among them who were skilled in other trades. These trades were primarily essential to agriculture. Among these persons were blacksmiths, carpenters, harness makers, wagon and carriage makers, tanners and millers. Grain mills and sawmills were two of the earliest industries in the county. The women were also skilled in spinning flax and wool into cloth which was used in providing clothing and other household linens.

At first their meetings for public worship were held in their houses. The general practice was to rotate from one house to the next within a given community or district. This practice continued for several decades until they decided to build meetinghouses.

The oldest known Mennonite meetinghouse in America that still remains from this early era is the one at Byerland, several miles southwest of Willow Street. This log building is situated along the old road from the village of Baumgardner to Clearfield. The exact date of the erection of this building is not known, but early records place it about 1747.

Most of the older meetinghouses were built of logs. These served for a number of years and then were replaced with larger buildings of more permanent material.

All services were conducted in the German language and the books used were the Bible and hymnbook. The Bibles were usually the Luther or Froschauer translations. The hymnbook was the ancient *Ausbund* that was first published for the Swiss Brethren in 1564. The first printing of this book in America was made in 1742. The singing was always done by the congregation without the aid of instrument or choir.

When a bishop, minister or deacon was needed in a congregation, he would be ordained by lot from the congregation. No special training was needed for this ordination. A bishop had oversight of a number of congregations.

Mennonites were directly involved in the founding of two other religious denominations in Lancaster County during the eighteenth century. The first of these was the United Brethren Church, of which a Mennonite bishop, Martin Boehm, was one of the original founders.

Boehm was born near Willow Street, Lancaster County, on November 30, 1725. In 1753 he was chosen by lot to serve as minister in what is now the New Danville District of Lancaster Mennonite Conference. He was advanced to the office of bishop in 1759.

In 1767 he participated in a "great awakening meeting" in Isaac Long's barn just north of Landis Valley, where he met Philip William Otterbein and where the seed of the United Brethren movement was sown. Ten years later he was excommunicated from the Lancaster Mennonite Conference. He took a considerable number of Mennonites with him into the United Brethren movement.

In 1791 he built a chapel on his farm a short distance south of the village of Willow Street. His remains repose close by this little chapel, which still stands in a good state of preservation. In his later years he left the United Brethren Church and found his fellowship with the Methodists. His grave marker reads in part: "Fifty-four years he freely preached the Gospel to thousands in the vineyard of the Lord Jesus in Pennsylvania, Maryland, and Virginia, among many denominations but particularly the Mennonites, United Brethren and Methodists, with the last of whom he lived and died in fellowship."

The second group originated primarily by persons of the Mennonite Church was the River Brethren. The founding of this group is not as clear as the United Brethren. When Jacob Engle, a member of the Mennonite Church, was twenty-five years old, he was convinced that baptism should be by immersion. It appears that he counseled with the leaders of the German Baptist Church (now Church of the Brethren) on this matter. Just why he and his sympathizers did not affiliate with the German Baptist group is not certain. Instead they proceeded to do as the first Swiss Brethren and the first German Baptist did and baptized each other.

From the record of the life of Martin Boehm in the *Mennonite Encyclopedia*, we learn that he also had some influence in founding this denomination. A small segment of this group, known today as the Old Order River Brethren, continues, but after 1862 the larger body adopted the name Brethren in Christ.

For the purpose of history, the Amish are another branch of Mennonites. They separated from the Mennonite Church in Switzerland after the first Mennonites had come to America. The cause of the division began as a doctrinal dispute between Hans Reist and Jacob Ammann, both Mennonite bishops. The tension began in 1693. After the parties could not be reconciled, final separation took place in 1711. The followers of Jacob Ammann were first called Ammannites in Switzerland, but in America they were referred to as Amish.

When the Amish first came to America is not certain. There is some evidence that they could have been in the Northkill settlement in Berks County by 1737. All of the first known Amish settlements in America were in Berks County, Pennsylvania. The first settlement that had a bishop to which a date can be firmly fixed is the one near Hamburg, Upper Berne Township, Berks County. Bishop Jacob Hertzler came here in 1749, served as bishop in that community and others, and is buried on the old Hertzler homestead.

The first permanent community of Amish in America is known as the Conestoga settlement. This includes parts of Berks, Chester and Lancaster Counties. They first settled in the Berks County section of this area in 1760. Again, it is not·clear when the first families came over to the Lancaster County side, but there are records available showing that Bishop Hans Blank was living at Spring Garden, Salisbury Township, before 1780. In 1771 there were familiar Amish names listed in the tax records of the Cocalico-Denver area, but it has not yet been proven that these were actually Amish.

The Conestoga settlement continued to grow and become a strong and prosperous community. From here the Amish continued to move westward into other counties and states.

The Amish have always engaged primarily in farming or related occupations. They have also resisted change, and in many ways they still follow methods used by their forefathers. The most noticeable practice carried over from former generations is the cultivation of their land by the strength of the horse. Most of their family transportation is also by horse and wagon.

The Amish have retained the same pattern of public worship that was used by them from the beginning. Their worship services are all conducted in their houses or barns. This also includes the services for weddings and funerals. Almost all the groups that have seceded from the Old Order group have built meetinghouses for their public gatherings, but the Old Order have none.

Their services are still all conducted in the German language. In their regular worship services they have continued to use the *Ausbund,* which is the same book that the early Mennonites brought with them when they came to this country. By continuing to use this hymnbook, which was first printed in a smaller format in Europe in 1564, they have given it a total lifespan of well over four centuries—a longer lifespan than any other Protestant hymnal.

The Presbyterian Church

MRS. KARL M. RICHARDS

FOLLOWING THE IRISH REBELLION, the attempt to establish the Church of England over Scotland and the consequent persecutions drove many stalwart Presbyterians to seek refuge in the Province of Ulster.

Taxation, exorbitant rentals and the resulting poverty led about 1700 disgruntled, dissatisfied, sturdy Scotch-Irish to come to America to settle along the shores of Pennsylvania, Delaware and Virginia.

The first distinctively Presbyterian Church was organized in 1698 in Philadelphia, and the first Presbytery (Philadelphia) in 1705. The Presbytery was later divided into subordinate "meetings" or presbyteries by 1716.

In 1709, Robert Galt, first Presbyterian settler in Lancaster County, crossed the Octorara hills and settled in the Pequea Valley. Doubtless he was one of the organizers of the Pequea Church. Other immigrants from northern Ireland landed at New Castle, moved on to Chester and into Lancaster County.

Donegal Church is said to have been founded by Arthur Patterson, probably as early as 1721. Andrew Galbraith asked the Presbytery of New Castle to supply ministers for Chicken's Longus (Chique Salunga). Several supplies and part-time ministers were available until the Reverend James Anderson, from a church on Wall Street, near Broadway, New York City, was installed in

9

1727 as the first pastor of Donegal Church. Several succeeding pastors met with disgraceful conduct, one being charged with intemperance and another admonished and suspended by Presbytery, although the cause is not known.

The Reverend Colin McFarquhar, the fourth pastor, conducted a Classical School and preached at Columbia before the church was organized there.

It was during McFarquhar's pastorate that the congregation of Donegal surrounded the white oak tree standing near the east end of the church and pledged their allegiance to the cause of the colonies. McFarquhar frequently had offered prayers for the King of England, but, after a courier brought news that the British Army had left New York under Lord Howe to invade Pennsylvania, he and the congregation pledged their loyalty to the cause of liberty and the founding of a new nation in the western world.

The Presbytery of New Castle sent Licentiate Adam Boyd, a native of Ireland, to Octorara (Upper) and Pikquae (Pequea) to collect and organize congregations. Pequea was probably organized in the latter half of 1724. Boyd was so effective that a call was presented for his pastoral services, and he was installed at "Acterera" Meeting House. He also ministered to territory now occupied by the Middle Octorara, Leacock, Donegal and Bellevue churches, as well as outside the Presbytery.

During the pastorate of Alexander Craighead, Pequea church was a divided congregation, resulting from the preaching and traveling of George Whitefield. Pequea and Leacock were identified with the "New Side" Synod,

Donegal Presbyterian Church and Graveyard

and separated from Donegal Presbytery. They did not return to Presbytery until 1759.

The Middle Octorara Valley was settled by strict Scotch and Scotch-Irish Covenanters and Presbyterians. The first building was erected between 1730 and 1738, possibly jointly built and alternately used by Presbyterians and Covenanters. The oldest grave in the cemetery is dated 1732, indicating that the burying ground was in use prior to the church.

Many churches in the area either shared ministers, or the ministers would serve one church for a few years, then accept a call to a neighboring church. Such was the case of the first pastor of Middle Octorara, John Thompson, who preached only two years, then accepted a call to Chestnut Level.

The second pastor, Thomas Craighead, had supplied at Middle Octorara until he accepted a call to the Pequea church in 1733. In 1734, Alexander Craighead, son of Thomas Craighead, was received into Donegal Presbytery and in 1735 was called to Middle Octorara. He was a zealous promoter of the "Great Revival" of George Whitefield and accompanied Whitefield through Chester County, making the woods ring with songs of praise. He claimed that ministers should not be confined within one congregation but should roam as evangelists wherever and whenever they wished. Thus began the schism of the "New Side" and the "Old Side." In 1740, Craighead was suspended from Presbytery. His ministry closed in 1741 when he went to Virginia, where he continued to render valuable service to his church.

It is worthy of note that from 1727 to 1965, Middle

Octorara had only nine pastors. Many of them stayed thirty, forty or fifty years, but there were also forty-four years of its history when supply pastors sent by Presbytery ministered to the congregation.

The church organized under the name of Chestnut Level probably dates back to 1717. The original church was located by the cemetery near Centreville about a mile east of Chestnut Level. A chestnut-covered plain overlooked the Conowingo Valley, giving the town its name. Mt. Pleasant was the original name of the village of Chestnut Level.

The first pastor of the congregation was the Reverend John Thomson, who began his work in 1732, the year in which Donegal Presbytery was organized. The present church building was erected on land in Drumore Township deeded to the church in 1760 by William Ritchey. His grant had come from William Penn's heirs. There are two traditions concerning the erection of the building, the first that the walls were erected in 1765 and the building completed in 1767. The other is that the walls were erected during the Revolutionary War and stood for quite some time as there were no men left in the area to complete the building.

Exact date of organization of the Little Britain Church cannot be determined, but it is thought to be sometime between 1732-34. If organization was that early, it must have been served by supplies for thirty years. Some members who were dismissed from Chestnut Level helped form the nucleus of Little Britain's congregation. Little Britain and Middle Octorara informed Presbytery in 1760 of a plan to unite, sharing a minister and his salary. In 1767, five years after Mr. James Hunt had been

13

installed at Little Britain, the congregation presented Presbytery with the request that the pastor-congregation relationship be dissolved, citing the following reasons:

> He preached too few times
> Visited only one family in four years
> Was late for services
> Had private interviews with those whom he desired.

Several ministers declined to accept calls to Little Britain, and for thirty-seven years, until 1803, Little Britain was dependent upon supplies.

Donegal Presbytery was organized on September 21 1732. The original territory was Lancaster County, but missionaries extended to "back parts of Virginia," Maryland, and North and South Carolina.

The churches in Donegal Presbytery at the time of its organization were:

> Chestnut Level
> Donegal
> Little Britain
> Middle Octorara
> Pequea

Geographical lines were loosely drawn in those days. Some ministers were received into Donegal Presbytery but labored in churches of New Castle Presbytery (Upper Octorara and Pequea). Nottingham and Lower Octorara were outside Donegal Presbytery, but the minister (William Orr) belonged to Donegal.

From 1741 to 1758, the Presbytery was divided into the Old Side Synod and the New Side Synod. The schism was based on questions of formalism in church structure, order and worship.

When the Gospel was first preached in what is now Leacock Church cannot be ascertained. The Reverend David Evans, native of Wales, was sent by the Presbytery of New Castle to Octorara, Forks of the Brandywine, Conestoga and Donegal as a missionary to the area in 1720. It is quite probable that he was the first Presbyterian preacher to officiate in that region and may have held the first regular services at Pequea (1724). This also may have led to meetings at Leacock before there was an organized church there. From 1741–50 the Leacock congregation obtained occasional supplies. Pequea and Leacock joined the New Side Synod and moved from Donegal Presbytery to New Castle Second Presbytery. They returned to Donegal Presbytery in 1759, when the schism was healed. In 1786 the Presbytery of Donegal divided into two Presbyteries, the Presbytery of Baltimore and the Presbytery of Carlisle. The Old Presbytery of Donegal ceased to exist.

The historic old Muddy Run Church is situated on the road from Rawlinsville to Holtwood in Martic Township. The land on which the church stands was patented in 1742 to David Jones, John Marshall and William Andrews, and a log house built the same year. Difficulties with the Indians at the time of the French and Indian War caused many settlers to migrate to South Carolina. Tradition holds that the meetinghouse was burned by marauding Indians. The second meetinghouse, also of logs, was erected in 1760. By this time also the Indian threat had subsided somewhat and the remnant of the congregation felt justified in commencing again. This log structure stood until 1820, when the church was replaced by a stone structure.

While the first recorded date is 1742, there were, without doubt, religious services held in the vicinity of Muddy Run for some time prior to that date at some settler's home or in a tent. These were most likely conducted by ministers who traveled from place to place. The Reverend John Cuthbertson, the first Covenanter Minister in America, records in his diary that he preached in the Muddy Run Meeting House on October 2, 1751, just two months after landing in America. The graveyard, at the rear of the Church, is well kept and contains graves dating from 1754.

The Octorara Covenanter United Presbyterian Church had its beginning between 1751 and 1754, probably in 1753. The first church was built in 1754 on six acres of ground and stood for ninety-five years.

In April, 1760, the Lancaster Church asked permission to secure supplies. Services for the First Church were originally held in the court house in Center Square. Governor Hamilton in 1763 donated a piece of ground on which to erect a church edifice. From the time of its organization until 1769, various supplies filled the pulpit of First Church.

Cedar Grove and Pequea Presbyterian Churches joined in worship, perhaps prior to 1775. The Presbyterians did not worship with the denominations already in this locale, but crossed the Welsh Mountains every Sabbath to worship with the Pequea congregation. At last the congregation selected a site near Blue Ball, erecting a platform for the minister and seats for the congregation, and it was called "The Run" as early as 1775. In 1785 the present site in a grove of cedar trees was chosen. In 1787 the first church building was erected, doubling during the week as a schoolhouse.

Despite the rigors of weather, distances of travel, and problems of establishing churches, homes and settlements, many ministers lived long, useful years. Those having pastorates of twenty years or more and dates on which the pastorates began are as follows:

Centre	1785	Rev. George Luckey	34 years
Chestnut Level	1771	Rev. James Latta, D.D.	30 years
Donegal	1748	Rev. James Tate	26 years
Hopewell	1793	Rev. Robert Cathcart	41 years
Lancaster First	1781	Rev. Hathaniel W. Semple	41 years
Leacock	1781	Rev. Hathaniel W. Semple	41 years
Middle Octorara	1781	Rev. Hathaniel W. Semple	41 years
Pequea	1751	Rev. Robert Smith, D.D.	42 years

Most ministers were well-educated and were willing and eager to give of their time to caring for the education and well-being of the young of their "flocks." They began the educational process by instructing a few students at a time, then founding classical schools in connection with their pastorates.

In the ensuing years only two of the ten congregations which had their beginnings in the eighteenth century dissolved (Muddy Run and Octorara). To the remaining eight have been added ten more; consequently, today there is a total of eighteen Presbyterian congregations in Lancaster County with a total membership of 8,994.

The Church of the Brethren

CALEB W. BUCHER

THE CHURCH OF THE BRETHREN, or the German Baptist Brethren as it was known earlier, originated in 1708 in Schwartzenau, county of Wittgenstein, Germany. The first members were originally Reformed who were strongly influenced by the Pietist and Anabaptist movements.

Prince Henry of Wittgenstein was liberal in his acceptance of the Pietists and others living in his province. Until his death the new group grew to become a congregation of some size, but after his death it was subject to persecution. Consequently many of the group fled to Marienborn and Kreyfeldt.

In 1719, after internal strife and excessive persecution, a group led by Peter Becker migrated to Germantown where many of their Mennonite neighbors had already gone. Alexander Mack, one of the original eight and considered to be the founder of the church, remained in Friesland in Europe until 1729. Between the two migrations others joined the Germantown community.

From 1719 until 1723 the Brethren were unorganized in Germantown. It is supposed that they were busy getting settled in their new land, building homes and clearing land for farming. Others were establishing businesses in the town to which they had moved.

On Christmas Day, 1723, Peter Becker called the

group to a meeting in Germantown after a baptismal service in the Wissahickon Creek. Here they met for a love feast service, and the Germantown congregation was born. The following year all the male members of the congregation traveled to Bucks, Chester and Lancaster Counties, to meet with scattered Brethren.

A baptism and love feast service was held near Pottstown on November 7, 1724. Here the Coventry Church was founded with Martin Urner, Sr., as the elected minister.

Peter Becker then traveled to the Conestoga country where he preached and held a baptismal service and a love feast. The Conestoga congregation, now located at Bareville, was organized somewhere south of Ephrata. Thus the oldest congregation of the Church of the Brethren of Lancaster County, known as the Conestoga Church, was founded on November 12, 1724, with twelve members. Peter Becker was their non-resident elder. (An elder in the Church of the Brethren was the equivalent of a bishop in some churches.)

Conrad Beissel, among others, was baptized in the Pequea Creek by Peter Becker and shortly thereafter was ordained to the ministry. Later his views regarding worship on the Sabbath instead of on Sunday caused division within the church. He established the Cloister community in Ephrata, where he was joined by others from the Conestoga and the Germantown congregations.

Alexander Mack, the founder of the church in Europe, arrived in Germantown in 1729. He and Peter Becker tried to resolve the existing differences but finally agreed to let the trouble be settled by a vote of the congregation. Eleven members decided to follow Beissel and twenty-

19

seven remained with the Conestoga congregation. This council meeting was held on Michael Frantz's farm near Millway.

Michael Frantz was elected the first local elder of the Conestoga congregation. After his elevation from the ministry to the eldership he served the church until his death in 1748. During Michael Frantz's ministry the congregation grew from twenty to two hundred members.

Michael Pfautz, second local elder, came from the Palatinate in 1727 and was baptized into the Conestoga congregation in 1739. In the first year of his eldership (1748), fifty-seven persons joined the church.

As the congregation grew in numbers the members moved farther from the location of the church. To serve as many as possible the congregation was divided in 1772 into the White Oak and the Conestoga congregations.

From these two eighteenth-century churches have grown all of the Brethren churches of Lancaster County as well as those in York, Dauphin, Lebanon and Berks Counties.

The Religious Society of Friends

PAUL L. WHITELY

THE RELIGIOUS MOVEMENT first known as "Children of Light" and later "Friends in the Truth," sometimes in derision called Quakers, and now officially known as The Religious Society of Friends, was a part of a larger mystical movement that belongs to the seventeenth century. The founder, George Fox, born in Fenny Drayton, Leicestershire, England, in 1624, was the son of Christopher Fox, a weaver by occupation, and often referred to by his neighbors as "Righteous Christer." George Fox was reared in a strict Puritan environment, and it is said that this "serious and delicate" child was little given to play. He had little formal education, but by virtue of his good intellect and self-discipline he attained extensive learning.

Although William Penn, one of the prominent early converts to Quakerism, came to America in 1682, the establishment of Friends Meetings and meetinghouses in Lancaster County belongs primarily to the nineteenth century. There were, however, a few meetings established in the eighteenth century. For example, one of the early meetings was the Sadsbury Preparative Meeting (in Quaker parlance), which was set up about 1724. In 1744, or thereabouts, fifty-six acres of land, one mile north of Christiana, was purchased from Richard and Thomas Penn. In 1747, a burial ground was plotted and a new

21

stone meetinghouse, still standing, was erected. This meetinghouse was vacated in 1903, and a new meetinghouse was erected in the borough of Christiana.

In 1728, Robert Barber, Samuel Blunston, John Wright and their families, from Chester County, settled in Columbia near which they had purchased one thousand acres of land. It is assumed that they held meetings in their homes at first, though a meetinghouse of square logs was built very early. After 1751, the meeting was under the care of Lampeter Meeting and was known as Wright's Ferry Meeting.

In 1758, a log meetinghouse was built on Union Street near Lane Avenue. It was used until 1812, when a red brick house was erected on Cherry Street.

Lampeter Preparative Meeting was located in Bird-in-Hand in East Lampeter Township. In 1732 it became known as the Leacock Preparative Meeting. As early as 1732, a log meetinghouse was built on a plot known as "Varman's Land." In 1790, a red brick meetinghouse replaced the log house. Though still standing, it is no longer used as a place of worship.

Established in 1753, a meeting in Lancaster was located on South Queen Street between Vine and German Streets. A brick house was built in 1759. The Lancaster Meeting did not flourish for long, and was disbanded in 1802.

Finally, Eastland Meeting, located in Little Britain Township, was established in 1796. Though meetings were held at first in a log structure, a more desirable meetinghouse was built in 1803. The story of other Friends meetings in Lancaster County belongs to the nineteenth century.

The United Church of Christ

JAMES E. WAGNER

WHEN THE UNITED STATES OF AMERICA in 1976 is cele-
brating the 200th anniversary of the Declaration of Independence, congregations of the United Church of Christ
in Lancaster County and elsewhere throughout the nation
will already a year previously have celebrated the 250th
anniversary of the formal beginnings of one major constituency of the present denomination.

The former Reformed Church in the United States (the
name of this constituency prior to the union of 1934) usually dates its beginning back to October 15, 1725, when
an observance of the Lord's Supper or Holy Communion
according to the German Reformed order was held for the
first time on these shores. It took place in the vicinity of
what is now known as Falkner Swamp United Church
near Boyertown, Pennsylvania.

From Philadelphia in 1732, a report was made to the
Reformed Synods of Holland describing the situation
among the early German immigrants:

> We think there are altogether fifteen to sixteen
> thousand German Reformed in Pennsylvania,
> but these people live scattered over more than
> three hundred miles of territory, and there are
> no churches in the land. We have thus far only
> two regularly called ministers. . . . Most of those

who come here are compelled to sell themselves for their passage money, and also their children, who generally must serve until their twentieth year. . . . We have no candidates at all for the ministry, and only a few school teachers. . . . During the past year (1731) nearly 4000 souls arrived in ten ships. By far the smaller number had any means, and the most of them had to be sold for their passage money. . . . When these people have served out their time, they are just as poor as when they first arrived, and it takes a long time until they contribute anything to the church.

To get a clear glimpse of the Lancaster County beginnings, one should note that references to Conestoga—variously spelled "Canastoga" or "Chanastocka"—refer not to the present village of Conestoga southwest of New Danville, but to the Conestoga Valley and north and east of it.

The German Reformed story in Lancaster County apparently goes back almost to the beginning of the eighteenth century. The late Reverend Fred D. Pentz, former pastor of Salem (Heller's) Church near Leola, wrote that "as early as 1712 members of the Reformed Church came into this section of Pennsylvania, now known as the Conestoga Valley, then as the 'Canastoga region'."

And the story is a profoundly moving illustration of how a devout and concerned layman, "without benefit of clergy," can exercise the evangelistic and pastoral genius by which the Christian Church has been preserved and promulgated through the centuries.

About 1721 (or shortly thereafter) John Conrad Tempelman, a tailor by trade from Heidelberg, Germany, emigrated with his family to Pennsylvania where he settled in Conestoga Township. He was about thirty years old, having been born in 1692. In a letter dated February 13, 1733, addressed to the Synods of North and South Holland (which had ministered to refugees in the earlier stage when they were fleeing from inhospitable areas of Germany and France), Tempelman wrote:

> The church at Chanastocka (Conestoga) had its origin in the year 1725, with a small gathering in houses here and there, with the reading of a sermon and with song and prayer, according to their High German Church Order upon all Sundays and holidays, but, on account of the lack of a minister, without the administration of baptism and the Lord's Supper.

That phrase "lack of a minister" illustrates in the Lancaster County German Reformed story the way legal tradition eventually gave way to what was felt to be a deeper religious need based on the New Testament, For, according to Reformed Church historian Dr. William J. Hinke, "on September 8, 1732, Tempelman baptized Susanna, daughter of Henry Bauman and his wife Catharina, nee Doerr, in Earl Township," and that act, says Dr. Hinke, "may be regarded as the beginning of Tempelman's ministerial career." For thirty-five years he continued his labors, organizing new churches as circumstances fa-

25

vored, highly spoken of all the while, but it was not until October 21, 1752, when, with the approval of the Fathers in Holland, Tempelman was finally ordained.

But to return to the beginning of the story and Tempelman's reluctance to exercise sacramental functions, he and the little congregation which we now know as Salem (Heller's) had heard of the work of that schoolmaster (also as yet unordained), John Philip Boehm, who had conducted that historic October 15, 1725, observance of the Lord's Supper near Boyertown. Tempelman and his flock invited Boehm to visit them, which he did, and to them also administered the Holy Communion on October 14, 1727, for the first known time in the Conestoga Valley according to the German Reformed order.

By the fall of 1730, another Palatinate German, John Peter Miller (Mueller), arrived. Before long he got himself ordained by the Presbytery of Philadelphia and for a little while served the New Goshenhoppen Church at what is now East Greenville, but by 1733 had joined Tempelman in the Conestoga Valley.

In the 1733 letter Tempelman wrote to the Synods of Holland, reporting that he was serving three churches: Salem (Heller's), Cocalico (i.e., Ephrata) and Lancaster; while the new man, Miller, was serving Muddy Creek (now Peace Church, Swartzville), White Oak (now Jerusalem Church, Penryn) and Zeltenreich's (now Zeltenreich-Mt. Tabor). By 1735, however, Miller had joined the German Seventh Day Baptists, taking with him some Lutheran and Reformed families from Dolpihacken (Tulpenhocken), and before the end of that year he himself entered the newly-opened Cloister at Ephrata.

Tempelman, by contrast, is not only credited with

founding or serving seven congregations in his early ministry, but, after relocating in what is now Lebanon County in the late 1730's, continued to serve congregations there until in the late 1750's, declining eyesight compelled his retirement. He is believed to have died in 1761, and is buried at Tempelman Hill, near Rexmont, close to where he had lived in Lebanon County. This faithful tailor, who founded and served the earliest German Reformed congregations in Lancaster County, is declared by Dr. Hinke to have been "without question the most important early Reformed minister in the Lebanon Valley," and credited with having ministered to seven congregations in each of the two counties.

By the time the Declaration of Independence was being signed and our Nation born, at least twelve of the congregations still members of the present Lancaster Association of the United Church of Christ were already in existence:

Penryn, Jerusalem Church, 1723; Leola, Salem (Heller's), 1725; New Holland, Zeltenreich's, 1728; Ephrata, Bethany Church, 1730; New Providence, Zion, 1730; Swartzville, Peace Church, formerly known as Muddy Creek Reformed, 1731; New Holland, St. Stephen's, relocated from Zeltenreich's about 1799–1800, but claiming the Zeltenreich's date, 1732; Lancaster, First, 1736; Elizabethtown, Christ Church, 1745; Reinhold's, Swamp Church, 1749; Maytown, Maytown Reformed, 1765; and Manheim, St. Paul's 1769.

There was a large number of staunch patriots among the German Reformed ministers and people. A notable example was the Reverend John Conrad Albert Helffenstein, pastor of the (First) Church at Lancaster.

In January, 1776, the Reverend John Conrad Helffenstein came to the pastorate in which he served until 1779. He was an enthusiast for the Revolution, although himself but newly come from Germany. He preached a number of fiery sermons to the soldiers and new recruits. He also preached to the Hessian prisoners, taken captives at Trenton and confined at Lancaster, but his sermons to them can scarcely have been comforting, since he chose such texts as Isaiah 53:3, "Ye have sold yourselves for naught, and ye shall be redeemed without money."

Zion Church, Brickerville, where there is no longer an active congregation but which still serves as a focus of historical interest, traced its organization to 1747, and the first church building was erected about a year later. During the Revolutionary War the original church building was used as a hospital for soldiers. A number of these died during their stay in the old church and are buried in the congregation's cemetery. Unfortunately, the graves of these patriots are not marked.

The revivalistic movement of the latter 1700's and the early 1800's gave birth to a number of vigorous new denominations. One of them was the Evangelical Church led by Jacob Albright. Another of these was the United Brethren Church, in the origins of which probably the most outstanding leader was the Reverend Philip William Otterbein who had been pastor of First Reformed Church, Lancaster, 1752–58. These two new denominations eventually merged to become the Evangelical United Brethren Church and, more recently in another major merger, part of the United Methodist Church. The third of these revival-born denominations is the Churches of God in North America which was organized by the

The Old German Reformed Church, Lancaster

Reverend John Winebrenner, pastor of Salem Church, Harrisburg, from 1820 until three years later, when he took part of that congregation with him to establish the first of the Churches of God group.

The effect of this revival movement on the Reformed Churches was not only that many of their members joined one or another of the new groups, but the emphases of the new groups on the necessity of personal religious commitment and the centrality of the Bible had a healthy impact on what by then had become a somewhat formal and lifeless characteristic of the older Lutheran as well as Reformed churches.

The Lutheran Church

HAROLD D. FRY

WITH THE EXCEPTION of Holy Trinity Church in Lancaster, all other Lutheran churches in eighteenth-century Lancaster County were rural or located in small settlements. Moreover all of these (again with the exception of Trinity Church) were "union churches"; that is, they shared property with other denominations—usually the Reformed, or present-day United Church of Christ. The members of these churches came almost exclusively from Palatine Germany.

Among the first German immigrants to arrive in America were many who had sufficient means to pay for their transportation. This group became smaller and smaller as the price for transportation rose. As a result the custom developed for immigrants to sell their services as indentured servants for a certain period of time—usually three to five years—to someone who would pay for their transportation.

The colonists who left for America were not soon forgotten by relatives and friends who remained at home, nor were they entirely neglected by their former spiritual shepherds. Various missionary societies were formed in Europe among different denominations to meet the need for pastors and to give financial support to churches in America. Among these was "The Society for the Promotion of the Knowledge of Christ in Foreign Parts" with which the Lutheran Church on the continent was connected. Prominent in this society were the Reverend Dr. Ziegenhagen, Lutheran Chaplain at the Court of St. James, and the Reverend Dr. Urlsperger, his assistant and later pastor of the St. Anna Lutheran Church in Augsburg, and Francke of the University of Halle which was under Lutheran management. It was from this latter place that Henry Melchoir Muhlenberg was sent to America. Muhlenberg was the clergyman who, after arriving on November 25, 1742, organized one congregation after the other and ultimately became known as "The Patriarch of the Lutheran Church." A few others had preceded him, but he did more than anyone else to unite Lutherans into formal organizations.

Colonial Lutheran Churches in Lancaster County included Holy Trinity, Lancaster, 1729; Emmanuel, Brickerville, 1730; Zeltenreich's (later Trinity), New Holland, 1730; Muddy Creek (near Adamstown), 1733; Bischoff's, Donegal, 1743 (later removed to Elizabethtown, 1771), Beaver Creek (later St. Michael's, Strasburg, 1748; White Oak (now St. Paul), Penryn, 1752; Bergstrasse (near Ephrata), 1752; Zion, Manheim, 1761; St. John, Maytown, 1767; and Christ, Elizabethtown, 1771.

In and about "Hickorytown" prior to 1730, when it was laid out as Lancaster, there were many German Lutherans. These received pastoral care from John Caster Stoever, Jr., a traveling missionary whose ministry to them began in 1729. Another of these traveling missionaries was John Christian Schultze, who became the first regular pastor in 1742. The first church, built of logs, was replaced in 1738 by another one on the site where Trinity Chapel stands. A walnut railing enclosed a

31

stone altar, above which rose the pulpit reached by ascending thirteen steps. On this pulpit stood the sand-glass measuring an hour and a half, the expected minimum time of a sermon. As early as 1746, Henry Melchoir Muhlenberg began visiting Lancaster to help the congregation.

In 1761 the present Lutheran Church of the Holy Trinity was built from brick brought from England as ballast in ships. As early as 1744, Trinity Church had a pipe organ, a rare possession in those days, so rare that a British prisoner in 1778 sent back a description of it to London.

From the steeple of Trinity Church swung the "Liberty Bell of Lancaster," originally brought from England to Ephrata for use in the Cloister there. It was sold to Trinity Church because the humble Cloister brethren objected to the proud display of so fine a bell. This bell was rung for the assembling of the Continental Congress dur-

Holy Trinity Lutheran Church and Chapel, Lancaster

ing its sessions in Lancaster in September, 1777, while the British were occupying Philadelphia.

Through the years Trinity Church was served by outstanding clergy, perhaps the most prominent of which was the Reverend Gotthilf Henry Ernst Muhlenberg, son of the patriarch, who came in 1780. Dr. Muhlenberg was a profound scholar, proficient in Greek, Latin and Hebrew. He also excelled in the natural sciences, especially in botany, and has been called "The American Linnaeus" by those who compare him to the Swedish scientist who classified plants and discovered cross-pollenization. Dr. Muhlenberg strongly advocated advanced education, and his efforts led to the establishment in 1787 of Franklin College (later Franklin and Marshall) of which Muhlenberg became the first president. All preliminary meetings and formal organization of the college took place in Trinity Church.

While the Nation was mourning the death of George Washington, Pennsylvania suffered the loss of Thomas Mifflin, her first governor, one of three Quaker generals in the Revolutionary War. He died in Lancaster, then the state capital, and was buried just outside the west wall of Trinity Church, a simple tablet marking his resting place.

Another prominent Lutheran Church in Colonial times was Emmanuel Church, Brickerville, formerly known as the Evangelical Lutheran Church in Warwick Township. This church dates from 1730. Ground for the church was purchased directly from the Penns for the sum of four pounds, nine shillings, nine pence (about $22). The tract contained twenty-nine acres. The church building was constructed of logs and was of considerable size. It was used as a hospital for the sick and wounded soldiers of the

33

Continental Army following the Battle of Brandywine. George Washington is said to have worshipped in this building during his visits to the "Elizabeth Mansion" with "Baron" and Mrs. Henry Stiegel, the product of whose iron mines nearby were of material assistance in winning the Revolutionary War. The "Baron" and his wife were members of the congregation and members of the vestry, and the "Baron" represented the congregation as lay delegate at the convention of the Ministerium of Pennsylvania at Philadelphia in 1762.

Because of the activities of "Baron" Henry William Stiegel, the stories of the Brickerville and the Manheim congregations are closely united. While serving on the vestry of the Brickerville Church, the "Baron" with several associates laid out the village of Manheim. In this village lot number 220 was set aside "Church Lott. No price." This took place in 1762. During the following year Stiegel erected an imposing red brick house, on the second floor of which he set aside a large hall for divine worship, furnished with seats, an organ, and a pulpit. Tradition has it that Stiegel himself preached to his employees and his German neighbors in the village. During this time Stiegel lived principally at his Elizabeth iron works and maintained active interest in the Brickerville Church. In 1765 in addition to the iron works, Stiegel erected a glass factory in Manheim, importing glassblowers from abroad.

Because of his deep interest in church affairs, Mr. Stiegel made the acquaintance of Henry Melchoir Muhlenberg. On September 18, 1769, Reverend Muhlenberg accompanied Stiegel to Manheim where, according to Muhlenberg's Journal, "A fair number of German people had assembled. After a service the male members united to organize a little congregation, wrote down their names, elected two of their number as deacons, and petitioned for occasional ministrations from Lancaster."

Another journal entry, under date of November 4, 1770, recounts a journey made after a service at the Brickerville church:

> Manheim lies 9 miles away and one must go over hill and dale on rough country roads to get there. Since riding is becoming hard and laborious for me, the iron master ordered out his coach and drove me hither. The nature of a journey in country wagons and coaches here is to be sharply distinguished from riding in European sedans. For two hours we were so shaken, bumped, jolted, and wrenched, that not only the material out of which the coach was constructed, but also our nervous systems, creaked and cracked.

Three weeks later, Muhlenberg sent his son the Reverend Frederick Augustus Conrad Muhlenberg, who had just completed his studies in Germany, to become the pastor. It was during this pastorate that the "Church Lott, no price" was officially deeded to the congregation. The deed which conveyed the lot from the Stiegels to their fellow Lutherans contained a clause which specified that there was to be paid to "Henry William Stiegel, His Heirs or Assigns in the month of June yearly hereafter the rent of One Red Rose if the same shall be lawfully demanded." This payment has been made annually.

The Jewish Faith

PAUL ROSENFELD

LANCASTER IS ONE of the oldest Jewish settlements in the state and in the country. As early as 1720, Jews are reported to have settled in Lancaster County in Schaefferstown, then a part of Lancaster County, and now in Lebanon County, a settlement now completely extinct. Although this Schaefferstown (then known as Heidelberg) group is less important in Lancaster County Jewish history than later groups, their cemetery was one of the oldest Jewish burying grounds in the American colonies.

The second Jewish colony in Lancaster County began around 1730 in the town of Lancaster itself. The leading figure of this period was Joseph Simon, Indian trader and merchant, and one of the prominent figures in Lancaster County history. A plot of ground was deeded to him in 1747 for a Jewish cemetery. This is still in use, and is maintained by Temple Shaarai Shomayim, one of Lancaster's three synagogues, as the congregation's burial ground. In the cemetery are buried Joseph Simon, the grandfather of Rebecca Gratz, and other early Jewish settlers.

Joseph Simon was undoubtedly the one who gathered together the first Lancaster Jews and assembled them for worship in his home. This early congregation called itself "The Society of Jews." The very old Ark used there was later presented to the American Jewish Historical Society. The Jewish Community in Lancaster in the 1740's and for more than a century, was not very large, consisting perhaps of no more than a dozen families. From 1804 to 1855 there was no interment in the cemetery. This would indicate that the Jewish population was so small that the living feared that their dead would not be cared for in the cemetery.

Commemorating the Tercentenary of the arrival of the Jews in America in 1654, Professor Fredric S. Klein of the Department of History of Franklin and Marshall College made the following pertinent observations concerning the Jews of Lancaster, who today number some two thousand individuals:

> Jewish history in Lancaster is a typical illustration of the great American story, extending from the days of the frontier fur trader, through the era of the immigrant and the traveling tradesman, to the period of the modern business or professional man who has become an integral part of the economic, social and cultural life of his community.
>
> Jews in Lancaster can take much pride in the long history of their ancestry in the affairs of this community. They were among the first of the pioneers; they were among the first of the many religious groups which settled here to enjoy Pennsylvania's religious freedom; one of their leaders, Joseph Simon, exemplified outstanding community citizenship in the days of the Revolution; their Lancaster congregation under his leadership seems to have been the first or-

37

ganized Jewish congregation in Pennsylvania; and the scores of young men and women who came here in the nineteenth century, bearing little with them but determination and hope, proved by their material success and their civic contributions that the American dream was a reality. ·

Tombstone of Joseph Simon (1712–1804) in Shaarai Shomayim Cemetery, Lancaster

The Episcopal Church

RALPH T. WOLFGANG

UNLIKE MOST OF THE IMMIGRANTS to Colonial Pennsylvania, the members of the Church of England were not seeking religious freedom. They came with the blessing of the Crown since they belonged to the Established Church, and King Charles II had written into William Penn's charter that any clergyman of the Church of England sent over by the Bishop of London at the request of at least twenty persons should not be harassed or molested. While most of the Church people were living in or near Philadelphia, a few scattered families had made their way west into Lancaster County before 1720.

The Church of England had been the official church of the empire since 1534. Though the separation from Rome had been prompted by purely political motives, it did not escape the influence of the Reformation. Its services were in English, and it encouraged its people to read the Bible in their native tongue.

The church in Pennsylvania was under the supervision of the Bishop of London. He never visited the colony but appointed representatives known as "commissaries." One such was the Reverend Thomas Bray, Commissary of Maryland, who saw the need to supply clergy in those colonies where the church did not receive public support. As a result of his urging, the Society for the Propagation of the Gospel in Foreign Parts, popularly known as SPG,

39

was chartered in 1701 to evangelize the Indians and Negroes and to minister to white congregations too small to support a clergyman. The first of their missionaries to be sent to Colonial Pennsylvania was the Reverend Robert Weyman, who arrived in 1719 and made his headquarters in Oxford, Chester County. In a report to the Society dated October 1, 1726, he stated that he had often traveled to Churchtown where, because no house was large enough to hold the congregation, he had preached to them under the shade of a large tree. Members of this little band of churchmen were largely Welsh, and by 1733 they were strong enough to build a church under the guidance of their Welsh missionary, the Reverend Griffith Hughes. They called their church "Bangor" after the name of their home Diocese. Thus, Bangor Church, Churchtown, is the first Episcopal Church in Lancaster County and the Diocese of Central Pennsylvania. Though set in the midst of the Amish country, it has remained in continuous service while other rural churches in Leacock and Paradise did not prove viable. Each spring pilgrims from the county visit Old Bangor for the Rogation Day service, and, on Memorial Day, friends from far and wide attend "Old Bangor Day" sponsored by The Friends of Bangor intent on preserving this historic church as a shrine.

Colonel James Hamilton, who, with his father, had laid out the borough of Lancaster in 1730, set aside certain lots for the use.of denominations who wished to build churches in Lancaster. Lots 34, 35 and 36 were reserved for the few members of the Church of England then resident in the borough. Lot 34 was to be used as a graveyard

Bangor Episcopal Church, Churchtown

and the other two for a church building. A ground rent of fifteen shillings was to be paid for the church lots, and this rent continued in force until 1843.

Though the churchmen were small in number, they exerted an influence out of proportion to their size. Among them was Thomas Cookson, first Chief Burgess of Lancaster, and Thomas Postlethwaite, proprietor of the tavern in which the Lancaster County court held its first sessions. Until 1744, Episcopal services were held whenever a clergyman was in the vicinity, but the people

41

were unorganized as a congregation. In 1744, the Reverend Richard Locke, a missionary of the Society, came to Lancaster quite by accident. He had been working in Bermuda and had sailed, as he thought, for Charleston, South Carolina, but his ship landed in Philadelphia. He made his way to Lancaster where the little band of churchmen prevailed upon him to stay with them and organize a congregation. This he did, and on October 3, St. James' parish was formally organized.

Since the congregation had no house of worship, services were held in the courthouse then located on Penn Square. A subscription was undertaken to raise funds to build a church, but the money came in so slowly that it was 1753 before the church could be occupied. It was a small stone church located on its present site at the corner of Duke and Orange Streets. Relations with Mr. Locke were unhappy, and he returned to England in 1748.

For the next three years, the congregation was without a spiritual leader; then the Society sent them the Reverend George Craig. Both he and Mr. Locke were licensed as missionaries to New Jersey and Pennsylvania. In actual practice, they served Bangor Church, St. James', St. John's Pequea, and a church on the frontier near York Springs in Adams County.

Relations with Mr. Craig were no more pleasant than with Mr. Locke. Both were English and out of sympathy with the American spirit of democracy. Conditions did not improve till the coming of the Reverend Thomas Barton in 1759.

Mr. Barton had an extensive American experience. Before his ordination he had taught in the Philadelphia Academy and, upon his ordination, had served the frontier churches in Pennsylvania. He had begun a fruitful work among the Indians who came to trade at Carlisle, and this work might have been highly successful had not the French and Indian War turned them from friends to enemies. He accompanied General Forbes on his mission to capture Fort Duquesne and, on his return, the Society sent him to Lancaster to try to bring peace to this troubled congregation.

His ministry in Lancaster began on Easter Sunday, 1759. For the next nineteen years he served the mission with distinction. Despite a frail body he not only served his people in Lancaster, Churchtown and Pequea, but he sought out church families beyond the bounds of his parish. It was he who held the first services in Columbia; occasionally he visited the people across the Susquehanna; and once, at least, he visited Reading.

The outbreak of the Revolution brought an end to this happy relationship. He considered himself bound by his ordination oath and his loyalty to the Society to pray for the King and the royal family. Since the influential members of St. James' were stout patriots, they would not tolerate such prayers. When independence was declared, Mr. Barton would not take the oath of loyalty to the new United States and so was restrained from holding public services. The windows were boarded up and the church closed till hostilities should cease. Meanwhile, Mr. Barton ministered to the sick and distressed in their homes. When General Howe evacuated Philadelphia in 1778, he got permission to accompany him to New York. His wife and family were not permitted to go with him, and they found shelter with parishioners in Churchtown. Worn out by the strain under which he had lived and by grief at

43

separation from his loved ones, he died in New York in 1780 at the age of fifty.

When England acknowledged the independence of the United States by the Treaty of Paris in 1783, any further help from the Society was out of the question, for its charter forbade it to work outside British dominions. Fortunately, St. James' was able to secure the services of a clergyman in the person of the Reverend Joseph Hutchins. He remained with the congregation for five years and got the parish back on its feet. With William Parr, Edward Hand and George Ross, he attended the convention at Christ Church, Philadelphia, which organized the Diocese of Pennsylvania. A year later, he attended the convention which elected the Reverend William White as first Bishop. He was a trustee of the newly established Franklin College and taught English there for a year. He returned to England in 1788.

Early the next year, the Reverend Elisha Rigg became Rector of St. James'. He was a young American and had just been ordained by Bishop White. He came to Lancaster an eligible bachelor and before the year was out had married the daughter of his Senior Warden, Judge Atlee. Like his predecessor, he was much interested in education and opened a Female Seminary. He resigned late in 1796 to become Rector of "Old Wye Church" on the Eastern Shore of Maryland. Until 1799, when the Reverend Joseph Clarkson became Rector, Mr. Hutchins, who had returned to Philadelphia was the interim pastor.

The story of the Colonial church in Lancaster County is the attempt to plant an English church in Pennsylvania Dutch soil. That it should have taken firm root is a notable achievement, but take root it did.

The Roman Catholic Church

EDGAR MUSSER

IN THE YEAR 1534, Inigo Lopez de Recalde, a Spanish nobleman, and six companions met in the crypt of the Church of St. Mary in Paris and formed the nucleus of a body of religious men who became identified as the Society of Jesus. De Recalde today is known as St. Ignatius of Loyola, the founder of the Jesuit Order.

From this small beginning the organization grew rapidly, spread over Europe and carried the Catholic faith as far as Japan and America. In the same year of 1534, while de Recalde and his companions were meeting in Paris, Jacques Cartier sailed into the Gulf of St. Lawrence and planted on a headland a huge wooden cross, to which he nailed the Arms of France. During the ensuing years other "voyageurs" came over to explore the American wilderness, among them Jesuit Fathers Jacques Marquette and Isaac Jogues.

Nearly forty years before the coming of Marquette to Canada, there arrived on the American scene some 200 emigrants from England, sent to colonize the Territory of Maryland for Cecil Calvert (Lord Baltimore) under the direction of his brother, Leonard Calvert. This was in 1634. With the colonists came two Jesuit missionaries, Fathers Andrew White and John Altham.

Others followed, and by 1640 the Jesuits, now acquainted with Indian language, were frequent guests of

45

the red men in their villages over a wide area. In the annual reports sent in to headquarters by the missionaries in the field, known as *Jesuit Relations*, it is recorded that the Conestoga Indians were visited regularly in their village before 1670, and instructed in the Christian religion.

In 1704 the Jesuits established a mission house in Bohemia Manor, on the Eastern Shore of Maryland, and named it the Mission of St. Francis Xavier. They moved into this new area because they had encountered many obstacles in the performance of their work while in lower Maryland. From Bohemia they began to journey into southeastern Pennsylvania, and during the 1720's visited the Philadelphia area, Conestoga (the name by which Lancaster County was then known), and Conewago in what is now Adams County.

Tradition says that Father Greaton, the first Jesuit missionary sent to Pennsylvania to work among the immigrants from Europe, had in his travels through this area become acquainted with an Irishman by the name of Thomas Doyle. Doyle had come from Maryland in 1727 and settled near "Hickorytown," an early name for what is now Lancaster. Father Greaton—so the story goes—had not been able to locate any Catholics within the confines of the town of Philadelphia during his visits there. To help him out, Doyle directed him to an old Irish lady in that town who was a Catholic. She was a relative of his by the name of Elizabeth McGawley, who lived along the road between Nicetown and Frankford. As a consequence of this information, Father Greaton in time established himself in Philadelphia and built the first Catholic church (St. Joseph's) there in 1733. He worked alone for twelve years, visiting Lancaster and Conewago periodically, until he was joined by Father Henry Neale, another English Jesuit, in 1741.

Father Neale, in 1742, received a grant of two lots in the town of Lancaster from James Hamilton, for the purpose of building a chapel. They were lots 235 and 236, located on the southeast corner of Prince and Vine Streets.

Up to this time the Catholics of Lancaster had received periodic visits from English-speaking priests only, sent here by their superior at Bohemia. Most of the Catholic residents of the Lancaster area were German immigrants, and because of the language problem that existed, an appeal was made to the Jesuit Provincials in Germany for German priests to come to America to minister to their countrymen in Pennsylvania. Two German Jesuits responded to the appeal and arrived at Bohemia, Maryland, in June 1741. They were the Reverend William Wappeler, S.J. and the Reverend Theodore Schneider, S.J. They were sent to Lancaster in July; came up the Chesapeake Bay, the Susquehanna River and the Conestoga Creek by boat (probably a rowboat), and became guests in the home of Thomas Doyle at the northwest corner of King and Water Streets.

Father Wappeler began at once to visit the Codorus (York) and Conewago, among other places, and arranged for the erection of small log chapels in those areas. Father Schneider worked toward the east—through the Berks County region, and into Philadelphia to minister to the Germans there.

The Lancaster mission territory was given the title "Mission of St. John Nepomucene." Somehow, from this evolved "St. Mary of the Assumption" as the name of the church. Perhaps it had that name from the beginning—nobody knows. St. Mary's Church (as a parish) was organized in July, 1741, and a rented house served as the first church. The location of that rented house has been forgotten over the years.

The granting of the two lots to Father Neale in 1742 resulted in the building of a log chapel in 1743, on the site of the present school building. It had been intended to erect a stone church, but the death of Father Wappeler's principal benefactor, Sir John James, of Crishall, Essex, England, caused a change in plans. Prominent among the founding members of the church were Thomas Doyle, John Hook and Roger Connor.

Father Wappeler, who was a native of Neuen Sigmaringen, Westphalia, Germany, remained in charge of the Lancaster mission seven years. His territory extended many miles in nearly every direction and, as did all early missionaries, he traveled in all kinds of weather; heat, cold, rain and snow. His territory included the present counties of Lancaster, York, Adams, Dauphin, Lebanon and Chester. In 1748 at the age of thirty-seven, because of failing health, he was compelled to turn over the six missions he had established to the man who accompanied him here seven years earlier, Father Theodore Schneider. He returned to Europe, where with the help of time and rest he regained his health and lived to reach the age of seventy. He died in September, 1781, at Bruges, Belgium.

Father Theodore Schneider was born in Gernsheim, Hessen, Germany, April 3, 1703. He received his early education in Speyer, and in 1718, when not yet sixteen years old, enrolled at Heidelberg University. At the end of one year he received his Bachelor of Arts degree; another year later he became a Master of Philosophy. On September 25, 1721, at the age of eighteen, he entered the Jesuit Order at Mainz. That he could have progressed so rapidly is almost unbelievable, yet the dates of his advancements are documented facts obtained from the archives of Heidelberg University. He became Professor of Philosophy at the university and was regarded as one of the foremost mathematicians of his day. In 1738 he was chosen *Rector Magnificus* of Heidelberg University, the equivalent of president in an American university. In 1740 he left the university to come to America and renounced a brilliant future in the learned circles of Europe to devote the rest of his life to laborious missionary work in this country.

When he took over Father Wappeler's responsibilities he did not relinquish the care of his own missions. Now he was the only Jesuit missionary left in the Colony of Pennsylvania; his predecessors had either retired because of declining health or, in Indian parlance, had "answered the call of the Great Spirit."

It had been the practice of both missionaries to visit each mission station in their respective territories once a month. Now that Father Schneider had to take over all of them, instead of appearing every four weeks, he had to lengthen the time between visits to eight or nine weeks. He continued this routine for four years, until June, 1752, when Father Ferdinand Farmer was sent to Lancaster to relieve him. Goshenhoppen (now Bally), in Berks County, was more like home again, and he was able to return to the routine of earlier years in his own territory. He died July 10, 1764. His remains were interred in the sanctuary of the little stone chapel he had built many years earlier, part of which has been preserved. Father Ferdinand Farmer, S.J., came to America in 1752. He was born in Weissenstein, Wurttemburg, Germany, October 13, 1720, admitted to the Jesuit novitiate at Lansparge in 1743, and was ordained around 1751. After his ordination he joined the English Province of the Jesuits. His original name was Andreas Steinmeyer, but like many other Jesuits, he adopted an assumed name in an effort to thwart the application of the English Penal Laws. However, the Jesuits were never impeded in the performance of their ministry in Pennsylvania—as they had been in Maryland—by anyone in governmental authority.

Father Farmer arrived in this country June 20, 1752, at the age of thirty-one and was immediately placed in charge of the Lancaster mission as resident pastor. A few months after his arrival in Lancaster, he established the Donegal Mission of St. Mary of the Assumption, near Elizabethtown. It was from this mission chapel that St. Peter's Church of Elizabethtown developed. The new name was adopted when the church was erected in 1799.

In 1757 Father Farmer reported to the governor of Pennsylvania that the number of Catholics in Lancaster County included: Germans, 108 men and 94 women; Irish, 22 men and 27 women, a total of 251. There were fewer than 2,000 Catholics in the whole of Pennsylvania, out of a population of about 200,000.

In 1758 he was transferred to St. Joseph's Church, Philadelphia, where he remained until 1786, the year of his death. He became the founder of the first permanent Catholic church in New York City, St. Peter's on Barclay Street, organized in 1785. He was a member of the

Philadelphia Philosophical Society and a trustee of the University of Pennsylvania. He was esteemed and welcomed in the most enlightened society of Philadelphia.

Father James Pellentz succeeded Father Farmer as resident pastor at St. Mary's. He, too, was born in Germany, January 19, 1727, entered the Society of Jesus in 1741 and took his vows in 1756. He came to the Mission of St. Francis Xavier from Europe in 1758 and from there was assigned to Lancaster.

When he arrived in Lancaster, Father Wappeler's little log chapel was still in use, but on the night of December 15, 1760, it was completely destroyed by fire. The fire obviously was of incendiary origin, and the burgesses of the town promptly offered a reward of twenty pounds to the person who would discover and report the guilty party.

In 1761 an additional lot of ground was acquired from Mr. Hamilton and work was started on a new church, which was completed in 1762. The new church, built of limestone, was erected over the place where the log chapel stood and was considerably larger. It was built in keeping with a custom that had been followed throughout the centuries, so that during the services the priest and congregation would be facing the East, where Jesus Christ was born, died and rose again. This second church lasted until 1881, when it was dismantled and replaced with the present school and convent.

In 1764 St. Mary's acquired a parcel of ground (Lot No. 234) on the northeast corner of Prince and Vine Streets, opposite the church. Tradition says it was given to the church with the purpose in mind that a school be erected on the lot, but the property was retained until 1887, when it was sold. In 1768 Father Pellentz was transferred to the Conewago Mission, which he served faithfully until his death in 1800.

Father James Frambach, from the Jesuit Province of the Lower Rhine, succeeded to the pastorate of St. Mary's in 1768. He had accompanied Father Pellentz to this country in 1758 and on arrival was sent to Conewago. He was stationed in Lancaster only a year and a half, and once the part-time services of Father Luke Geissler, of Philadelphia, were made available to the congregation at Lancaster, he returned to Conewago to cover the missions of western Maryland and northern Virginia. He died and was buried at St. Inigoes Mission, St. Mary's County, Maryland, in 1795.

Father Luke Geissler was the last of the German Jesuits to serve St. Mary's prior to the temporary temination of the Society of Jesus by Pope Clement XIV in 1773. He was born in Germany in 1735, entered the Jesuit Order in 1756 and came to this country in 1769. During the 1770–1774 period he divided his time between Lancaster and Philadelphia. Thereafter the restrictions imposed by war and suspicions made it unwise for him to visit that city.

After the Society of Jesus was disbanded in 1773, the Jesuits became secular priests, and there were no priests of that Order in Lancaster until 1807, by which time the Order had been reactivated.

In 1775 Father Geissler had a new organ built for St. Mary's Church by David Tannenburg, the famous organ builder of Lititz, Pennsylvania. This organ later was sold to the First Reformed Church of Lancaster and for many years was used in the Sunday School room of that church. Some years ago the pipes and manual were removed, but the panelled case was preserved, refinished and converted into a storage cabinet for miscellaneous church property. It is still in service.

Father Geissler was pastor of St. Mary's Church during the trying years of the American Revolution. Two members of the parish, Major John Doyle and Captain John Doyle, Jr., saw prominent service with Washington's Army. Another to answer the call to fight for independence was the prominent wheelwright, Michael Hook, a member of Company 7 of the 6th Battalion from Lancaster County. Caspar Michenfelter, active in church affairs at that time, also enlisted for military service, and there were others.

Father Geissler, during the time he was pastor of St. Mary's, built the first Catholic church in Carlisle, St. Patrick's, in 1784. He became very ill in 1786 and retired to Conewago, where he died August 16, 1786.

Old St. Mary's Roman Catholic Church, Lancaster

By the time Father Geissler reached the end of his missionary career, the Catholic people of Lancaster, as well as those in all the rest of southeastern Pennsylvania, had been under the spiritual care of the Jesuit Fathers for nearly sixty years. Without exception they were able and erudite men, who had foregone lives of comparative ease in Europe to come to America, much as today's missionaries go to distant lands, leaving behind them relatives, friends and all they cherish in their native countries. They were humble, zealous and tireless men, equipped with the qualities of strong character and priestly dignity, whose exertions toward keeping the light of faith burning in the pioneer days of Pennsylvania have set a standard of self-sacrifice and devotion to duty unsurpassed in the later history of St. Mary's Church.

The Moravian Church

CHARLES W. WIENEKE

FROM KUNWALD, BOHEMIA, to Herrnhut, Germany, to Georgia, to Bethlehem, Pennsylvania, to Lancaster and Lititz. Therein lies our Moravian lineage.

Beginning with a movement in the late fourteenth century when the practices of the established church were questioned by conscientious scholars of theology, a Bohemian priest named John Hus took up the call for a return to the principles of truth. For his refusal to recant his beliefs, he was condemned to death. His followers, convinced of his rightness, carried on his belief and one group at Kunwald formed a pre-reformation, "Protestant" church which they called the Brethren's Unity. In 1457 this church was formally organized.

Nearly sixty years later, in 1514, Martin Luther precipitated the Reformation. This event did not bring a tranquil period for the Unity, however, for the persecution, endured under the State Church prior to the reformation, continued. Under tolerant rulers the Unity flourished. Under intolerant rulers it suffered until finally, with one surviving Bishop (John Comenius) there was but a small number left, "a hidden seed," to attest to the Unity's existence at all.

In refuge, this vestigial group fled first to Poland and thence to Saxony in Germany carrying with it the traditions of a "free" religion derived from Hus, Comenius

55

and others. In Saxony, on the estate of Count Nicholas von Zinzendorf they found a haven. It is here that they became labeled "Moravians" after the area from which they had originally come. Under Zinzendorf's protection they established the community named Herrnhut. Here events occurred which led to a renewal of the Unity, and the impression which they made upon Zinzendorf led to his becoming one of their most influential leaders.

Concern grew for spreading the Gospel among heathen lands. The first Protestant missionaries went to witness to the slaves of the Virgin Islands in 1732. An attempt to witness to the Indians in the Georgia Colony of the North American continent failed, however. The work was transferred to Pennsylvania. In 1741 Bethlehem was founded as a center of activities. There being no established denomination in Pennsylvania at this time, the need for preaching to European (German speaking) settlers equalled the need for missions to the Indians. Therefore, this became a further challenge to the Moravians. With the idea of de-emphasizing denominationalism in favor of furthering vital religion, Zinzendorf promoted the idea of a union of all Protestant churches in Pennsylvania which he called the "Pennsylvania Synod."

To further this plan, thirty-one centers of itineracy were established. Lancaster became one such center, and a Union Chapel called St. Andrew's Chapel was built in 1746. Here, traveling ministers from various denominations, yet themselves sympathetic to the Synod idea, held regular non-denominational services. With the failure of the Synod idea for want of support from other denominations, a number of people who had joined the Moravians asked to become a separate congregation. It was thus that

Moravian Church, Lancaster (from old sketch)

the congregation in Lancaster was organized and began meeting in St. Andrew's Chapel. The chapel, located at Market and West Orange Streets, gave way to a larger structure in 1820. Although remodeled on several occasions, this building was the congregational home until 1967, when the church was relocated to the Eden site.

The Lititz Congregation was organized on February 9, 1749; however, a "gemeinhaus" (Community House) which served both as a school and residence for a minister, was erected in 1746. The school eventually evolved into two famous schools, The John Beck Academy, which went out of existence in 1865, and Linden Hall School for Girls, which will celebrate its 230th year in 1976.

Five years after the congregation was formally organized, John George Klein, who owned a farm of 491 acres upon which most of present-day Lititz is situated,

57

offered his farm as a nucleus for a Moravian Community. The land was transferred in 1755, and the name "Lititz" was conferred on the infant community. The present church building was erected in 1787.

The Lititz Moravian Church has been noted through the years for its missionary enterprises.

A second emphasis for which the Lititz Moravian Church has been noted both at home and abroad is in the field of education. Linden Hall, founded in 1746, is the oldest girls' boarding school in the United States. Graduates of the school live in every state of the Union and some twenty-seven foreign countries. The John Beck Academy—and its successor, the Beck Family School—for almost a century (1815–1895) made the best in education available to hundreds of boys and young men.

The third emphasis of the Lititz Moravian Church is in the field of music. Men of unusual musical talent have lived in Lititz. Their compositions, many still in manuscript form, only now are being recognized as foremost in early American music.

The United Methodist Church

JAMES Z. HABECKER

THE ROOTS OF THE UNITED METHODIST CHURCH go back to the conversion of John and Charles Wesley, which occurred in the year 1738. John followed his father in the priesthood of the Church of England. As a student at Oxford University, he and brother Charles organized student meetings for discussions of "the things of God." Eventually, a scheme of self-examination was agreed upon, and the hours of the day methodically organized so as to give time for Bible reading, meditation and prayer. This caused other students to refer to the group as "methodists" and "methodist societies."

While attending a meeting of the society in Aldersgate Street in London, John Wesley experienced his "evangelical conversion," and within six years, the Wesleyan movement took form. Wesley remained loyal to the church of his father, and had no intention originally of forming a new denomination. However, pulpits were often closed to these early groups, and field preaching became an important medium for spreading the gospel. Repeated efforts were made to provide ministers to the "methodists" within the established church, with little success. In 1771, Wesley sent Francis Asbury to America. Following the American Revolution, Wesley in 1784 ordained ministers to carry on the work in America.

The event officially chosen from which to reckon the

59

age of Methodism in America is the preaching of the first sermon by Philip Embury, in his own home in New York in 1766, although the Methodist Episcopal Church was not formally organized until the historic conference held at Baltimore on December 24, 1784, where both Dr. Thomas Coke and Francis Asbury were elected bishops. Interestingly enough, the Reverend William Otterbein, founder of the Church of the United Brethren in Christ, was present at this meeting.

Also, we must mention the name of the Reverend George Whitefield, praised by Ben Franklin in his *Autobiography,* who preached throughout the entire Atlantic seaboard during the middle eighteenth century. Whitefield was a pioneer in the Methodist movement, although he later separated from the Wesleyan Methodists. The *Pennsylvania Gazette* issues for the year 1746 make reference to Whitefield preaching in Lancaster County on several occasions. William Henry, Lancaster merchant and gunsmith, in his "Memoir," tells of hearing Whitefield preach in 1740, and was "greatly moved."

To complete the history of The United Methodist Church in America, one must review the beginnings of the United Brethren in Christ and Evangelical Churches, later, in union, known as the Evangelical United Brethren Church. Here, four great souls come to mind, each of whom had roots in eighteenth-century Lancaster County:

Martin Boehm (1725–1812); Philip William Otterbein (1726–1813); Christian' Newcomer (1749–1830); and Jacob Albright (1759–1808). These men, along with Wesley and Asbury, were contemporaries, and greatly influenced one another. Each was a Pietist, believing that

Christian faith demanded a personal conviction to Christ, and each rebelled against the formalism of his established church.

Martin Boehm, born in Pequea Township in Lancaster County, became a Mennonite preacher, chosen by lot, in 1756, and a bishop in 1759. Preaching in true pietistic tradition, he was strongly evangelical. He became active in the movement which later formed the United Brethren in Christ church. Later he was active for the Methodists.

Philip William Otterbein, born and educated in Germany, was ordained by the Reformed Church and came to this country in 1752 to work among the Germans in Pennsylvania. In the new world he became restless under the formalities of the old-world Reformed Church. He served as minister of the First Reformed Church in Lancaster and later accepted a call from the Baltimore Reformed Church—a separatist congregation—upon the urging of Asbury. This church, under the name "The German Evangelical Reformed Church," later joined in the formation of the Church of the United Brethren in Christ.

Christian Newcomer, born in Lancaster County of Mennonite parents, was baptized in the Mennonite faith. He became acquainted with Otterbein, and joined his Society. Eventually he was elected bishop in the United Brethren church. His journal contains a record of his travels and work covering the years 1795–1830, over a circuit from Philadelphia to Indiana, from Virginia to Canada. He crossed the Alleghenies forty-eight times. In Lancaster County, he preached at Zeltenreich's, Hellers and frequently at Boehm's.

Jacob Albright was born in the Oley Valley, near Colebrooksdale, Berks County. Confirmed in the Swamp Lutheran Church at New Hanover, he married in 1785, bringing his bride to a farm he had purchased southwest of Reamstown, in Brecknock Township. About the year 1792 he suffered the loss of six of his children in an outbreak of the plague. This tragedy seemed to mark the beginning of his religious zeal. He joined the Methodist Church and set up classes in religious study. By 1797, Albright traveled a circuit through Lancaster, Berks, Dauphin, and what today is Lebanon, Counties. Albright and Asbury are said to have discussed union of the Albright people and Methodists, but Asbury would not agree unless the Albright people learned to speak English. Albright continued preaching to the German people until his death in 1808, and only after his death would the religious classes he founded adopt the name Evangelical Association.

The eighteenth-century churches of the Methodists, Evangelical Association and United Brethren in Christ in Lancaster County consisted, for the most part, of early movements, although indications are that in 1781 a Methodist minister first visited the county, and a "Lancaster Circuit" was formed in 1782, with the Reverend William Partridge appointed minister. Martin Boehm's house and barn were the preaching places of Methodist itinerant ministers from 1775 to 1791, when the chapel was erected on land of the Boehm family. Plans for the chapel were furnished by Richard Whatcoat, one of John Wesley's helpers, and it is said that Boehm himself went to Wright's Ferry to fetch lumber for the chapel. Here at Boehm's, we are told, the early bishops of the church preached: Strawbridge, Abbott, Whatcoat and others, and of course, Francis Asbury. At quarterly meetings, the people came from Philadelphia and Maryland, and Boehm's was a center of influence. This historic first Methodist Church in Lancaster County is still standing, located just south of Willow Street, Pennsylvania.

Henry Boehm, son of Martin, became one of the first ministers to preach regularly at Boehm's. He writes in his journal, "Columbia was another of our preaching places. I was in this spot in 1791, when it was called Wright's Ferry. Methodism was introduced here near the close of the last century."

Benjamin Abbott came to Boehm's to preach in his home in 1780, and in his journal gives a vivid picture of the emotionally charged meeting which continued into the night and following morning. Abbott's account of his journey through Lancaster County is the first recorded

Boehm's Chapel as it looked in 1791

instance of regular Methodist preaching in the county. The news of this preaching mission attracted such attention in the church that in March 1781, Bishop Francis Asbury could write in his journal, "I have heard of a great work among the Germans towards Lancaster."

In addition to Boehm's, Soudersburg can lay claim to one of the earliest settlements in Methodism, which was introduced here in 1791. A house of worship was erected in 1802 on land sold by Joel Ferree to John Souders, and then conveyed to the Trustees, Jacob Souders, David Huss, and others. Bishops Asbury and Whatcoat visited here in 1803. While not occurring in the eighteenth century, it should be noted that Soudersburg was evidently important enough to have been selected as the site of the Philadelphia Conference in 1804, attended by 120 preachers.

Historians for the Church of the United Brethren in Christ trace the origin of their church to a meeting held in Isaac Long's barn, near Oregon, in Lancaster County, on Pentecost Sunday in 1766. (Some doubt exists as to correct date; it could be 1767.) Martin Boehm was a guest preacher on this occasion, and William Otterbein, pastor of Lancaster's First Reformed Church, was in the audience. Following the service, Otterbein was greatly impressed with Boehm's passion for Evangelism, and said to him, "Wir sind Brüder" (we are brethren). Other meetings followed, but this meeting signalled the beginning of a movement resulting in the formation of the United Brethren denomination. The first formal conference of this group was held in Frederick, Maryland, in 1800. At that meeting, the church was organized with Otterbein and Boehm elected bishops.

Isaac Long Barn, Landis Valley (from 1941 photograph)

John Wesley had a conviction that no single type of church government was set forth in the Scriptures, and that the manner in which churches were governed was of secondary importance. From the standpoint of extending Methodism throughout eighteenth-century America, this was an important fact, as it meant that Methodism was able to adjust its organization to the needs of a changing frontier. Thus, America provided a fertile field for the doctrines preached by the Boehms, Otterbein, Albright, Newcomer and others. Frontier life offered few opportunities for formal worship services, and the itinerant evangelist was in popular demand. Evangelistic meetings were attended with great enthusiasm by Christians of all faiths, as for example the meeting at Long's which drew Mennonites, Amish, Reformeds, Moravians, and others.

During the early formative periods, there are references to Asbury's group as "English Methodists" and to the Otterbein-Boehm-Albright groups as "German Methodists." These pioneer preachers on horseback represented a great revival movement in America; they attended each others meetings, often traveled together and preached together. Doubtless, had it not been for the language barrier, these groups would have united in Colonial times, instead of waiting until the year 1968, when the United Methodist Church was formed. The Methodist Church, along with the Evangelicals and United Brethren, can be said to have been born out of the Revolutionary War. Today, upon reflecting upon the terrible hardships endured by these itinerant preachers, with little or no salary, one wonders in awe what drove men such as Asbury, the Boehms, and others, to travel thousands of miles on horseback, through wilderness territory, to spread their version of the Gospel.

Among the German immigrants who came into Pennsylvania were very few clergymen, and prior to 1740, there was scarcely any religious care given these fundamentally religious people. The majority of the few clergymen who came to Pennsylvania were those with pietistic convictions. We are told that the period following the war was "the period of lowest morality in American history," and while such discouraging conditions were trying to those who came to Pennsylvania for religious freedom, and although the "Great Awakening" was largely an English movement, there were a few Evangelists who gave of themselves exclusively to the Germans. With all their cultural weaknesses, these early Pennsylvania Germans were at heart a religious people, and it was this group which made an important contribution to the rapid growth of Methodism—including the Albright and Otterbein groups—in eighteenth-century Lancaster County.

The Brethren in Christ Church

GLENN C. FREY

THE BRETHREN IN CHRIST cannot point back to an exact date of origin; neither their founders nor contemporaries made such a date a matter of record. Tradition placed their beginning in the late eighteenth century.

More adequate proof of the time of the Brethren's origin relates to knowledge about Jacob Engel, one of the founders. He was born November 5, 1753, and at age twenty married Veronica Schock. His father was Uhlrich Engel, a Mennonite, who emigrated from Switzerland with his family and arrived in Philadelphia, October 1, 1754, on the ship *Phoenix* out of Rotterdam. The Engels located along the Susquehanna River near the present town of Marietta in Donegal Township, Lancaster County, Pennsylvania. Following the death of both parents, Jacob, a minor child, appeared on June 26, 1724, in the Lancaster County Orphan's Court. He was then too young to have a legal voice in the choice of a guardian, so the Court appointed Peter Witmore of Manor Township, guardian of his person and estate.

Jacob Engel died in February, 1833, and is buried in the East Donegal Cemetery near Maytown, Pennsylvania. The inscription on his simple, sandstone grave marker reads:

Tombstone of the Reverend Jacob Engle
in Reich's Graveyard near Maytown

69

Here rests an old patriarch, whose labor in the
work of God was with diligence. Now he is in
his Father's land. Jacob Engel was his name.
His name now is much better. He lived and
died a true Christian. He brought his age to
three months, seventy-nine years, five days. He
now lives in eternal rest.

This inscription reveals the profound impression made by
his Christian life upon those who perpetuated his memory.

Since Engel did not reach his legal majority until
November, 1774, the Brethren obviously had not organized by that date; teenagers did not found churches in
eighteenth-century Lancaster County. Thus, 1775 is the
earliest approximate date for the Brethren origin, and
probability suggests a later date when Jacob Engel would
have been more mature.

In summary, the Brethren launched their movement
between 1775 and 1788. This time span includes the
dates given by all secondary sources which attempt to fix
the time of their origin; no source gives a specific date
earlier than 1778; none gives a specific date later than
1786.

Useful for an understanding of the early Brethren is
knowledge of the religious background from which they
came. Several of the early church leaders were Mennonite. As previously noted, the father of Jacob Engel was a
Swiss Mennonite. A mid-nineteenth-century source asserts that the early Brethren were sometimes called River
Mennonites, because some of their first ministers had
been connected with the Mennonites.

Evidence also suggests that the formulation of the theology and folkways of the founders owed more to German Baptist than to Mennonite influences. The reason for this cannot be established from current knowledge of Brethren origin.

All of the present churches tracing their heritages back to the Brethren, including Brethren in Christ, Old Order River Brethren (Yorkers), United Zion Children and Calvary Holiness, place primary emphasis upon personal, heartfelt Christian experience. The applicant for membership in any of these churches is always expected to testify to being "saved," that is, to profess the experience of a New Birth which brings to him assurance of forgiveness for his sins and a sense of peace in his relationship with God. Conversion in this sense is prerequisite for baptism as well as for church membership.

The roots of this emphasis upon personal Christian experience reach back into the eighteenth-century Pietistic awakening in Lancaster County. For persons well acquainted with these churches of Brethren heritage, the conversion experiences of Philip Otterbein and Martin Boehm and the conversion message which they preached have a familiar ring. Some sources assert that six of the early Brethren including Jacob and John Engel were converts of Martin Boehm.

A connection between Boehm's revivalism and the emergence of the Brethren is embodied also in United Brethren in Christ traditions. In 1841 Jacob Erb, a member of the latter group, produced the first known written account of the Brethren origin. Noting with satisfaction that the United Brethren in Christ had not been plagued with divisions characteristic of many religious

71

fellowships, he acknowledges one conspicuous exception—the River Brethren—and gives his version of how this occurred.

According to Erb, Martin Boehm founded "flourishing congregations" in Lancaster County on the Susquehanna River near Marietta, on the Conestoga northeast of Lancaster, and on the Becque (Pequea). Later, Erb says, the Susquehanna River congregation repudiated Boehm's leadership and became River Brethren. Erb's version of this transition is as follows:

> In those Districts there were, frequently, large meetings held, and when they came together, when anyone wished to introduce another to the brethren and to make known whence he was, he would say: this is a Conestoga brother, or a Becque brother, or a River brother, and hence they knew from what District he came. . . . As above mentioned, there were annually large meetings held at one or the other of those places, at which Boehm was always regarded as the Bishop or leader, and such a meeting was never appointed without his counsel. But in the course of a few years the brethren at the River took the liberty of appointing a meeting without consulting the brethren in the other districts, and without giving Boehm an opportunity of assenting thereto, nor was he invited to attend the meeting.

By arranging this unauthorized meeting, the River Brethren indicated their determination to break with Boehm's leadership.

Augustus Drury, a later United Brethren historian, embellishes the account by asserting that the Boehm congregations were principally Mennonites, but at the same time he refers to "diversity in the original elements of the (River) congregation." He points to Boehm's wide association with persons differing markedly from Mennonites and to Boehm's liberal views on baptism as factors disturbing the congregation. Drury concludes that about 1776 this Susquehanna River group became the "mother congregation" for the River Brethren.

A credible account of the Brethren, written later, mentions neither the Brethren's acceptance and subsequent rejection of Boehm's administrative leadership nor their secession as a Susquehanna congregation to form the Brethren. This account asserts that in the latter part of the eighteenth century "awakened" persons from various religious backgrounds who shared a common interest in the general cause of religion and in each other's personal edification "met in the capacity of a social devout band, from house to house, to make prayer and supplication for the continued influence of God's Spirit—out of these social circles, was organized the Religious Association, now commonly known as the River Brethren."

The assumption that Martin Boehm played a significant role in the emergence of the Brethren is not negated by questioning some of the details in the Erb-Drury account. As previously noted, two secondary writers state that Jacob and John Engel and several other early Brethren experienced Pietistic conversion under Boehm's ministry. More significant is the testimony of John Stehman, nephew of John Greider, who says that his uncle and the Engel brothers attended Boehm's meetings and for some time endorsed his preaching. Later, Stehman says, they began prayer meetings in their homes in Boehm's absence and eventually decided to form a church more like the primitive church than like his.

Undoubtedly, several of the early fathers responded positively to Boehm's preaching but drew back from commitment to churchly patterns which he espoused. They probably participated in Boehm-led "great meetings," a major technique of the Pietistic awakening, which brought together in spiritual fellowship persons of different backgrounds and faiths without severance of their denominational ties or the creation of what are now commonly thought of as congregations.

In summary, the data on the origin of the Brethren reveal that their early leaders responded positively to the call of the Pietistic awakening to a personal New Birth; they were "awakened" persons. Martin Boehm was one of the instruments by which this awakening emphasis was communicated to the Brethren movement. The experience of the New Birth advocated by the preachers of the awakening became a central concern of the Brethren; they held that this experience was essential for the beginning of a Christian life.

The Brethren's endorsement of a crisis conversion experience, coupled with their reservations about some of the views of its great Mennonite exponent, Martin Boehm, foreshadowed the development of their eclectic faith. With the Pietistic spirit of the religious awakening, which stressed the New Birth experience as normative for all Christians, they joined the deep concern for scriptural obedience which characterized the Anabaptist tradition. This concern emerged clearly in their desire to practice the scriptural ordinances faithfully and fully.

The ordinance of baptism played an especially crucial role in the emergence of the Brethren's movement, for their early leaders became convinced that trine immersion was the baptismal mode prescribed by the Scriptures. Once they reached this conclusion, their question was not whether to obey but how. They had two possible alternatives—either to secure the desired baptism at the hands of some ordained minister of an existing religious society or to take the bold step of baptizing each other.

Seen in historical perspective, the first alternative proved to be unrealistic. In Lancaster County only the German Baptists were trine immersionists and clergymen of other churches could have administered such baptism only by breaking the precedents of their respective faiths. Furthermore, the German Baptists did not make the New Birth a prerequisite for the ordinance of baptism as did the Brethren. The German Baptist position, therefore, made unlikely their administration of baptism on Brethren terms, while the Brethren position made equally untenable their acceptance of baptism on German Baptist terms.

Thus, the Brethren chose mutual baptism, and so crossed their Rubicon and launched a new religious society.

The founders of the new society referred to themselves originally as Brethren; probably they did not use the word in a formal, denominational sense. With the passage of

75

time, the United States branch of the movement became the River Brethren, although the date of their general acceptance of this name is unknown.

There is an obvious relationship of the River Brethren name to the Susquehanna River. Some sources assume that it simply identified the geographical location where the Brethren first appeared. Others relate the name to the tradition of a mutual Brethren baptism in the river. While such a river baptism is quite possible, the fact that Conoy Creek flows through the Jacob Engel homestead to the Susquehanna River suggests that the former stream may well have been the initial baptismal site.

Various sources suggest that the River Brethren name distinguished Jacob Engel and his associates from other societies referred to as Brethren.

Another explanation, and the one best supported by the sources, holds that the River Brethren name first developed as a distinction within the Brethren movement itself. There are two variants of this view. A mid-nineteenth-century source states:

> The appelation they assumed, is "Brethren," considering as Christ is their master, and that they, as his disciples, "are all brethren," Matt. xxiii.8; James iii.1. Several societies in different parts of Lancaster County were simultaneously organized: one near the Susquehanna River; another on Conestoga Creek. By way of local distinction, the latter were called the Conestoga Brethren, those on, or near Susquehanna, the

River Brethren, an appelation by which the society is now generally known, to distinguish its members from the German Baptists, or Brethren, first organized in Europe.

This quotation reveals that not all different explanations of the River Brethren name are mutually exclusive. In this explanation the name which originally met a need for a geographical distinction within the Brethren movement evolved later into a means of distinguishing the adherents of that movement from the German Baptists.

The Evangelical Congregational Church

RAYMOND S. REEDY

NOT THE LEAST IMPORTANT of the many valuable contributions which Europe has made to American civilization is that large group of people who emigrated from southern Germany between the years 1683 and 1755. Living in the Palatinate had become unbearable because of religious oppression; the constant state of war in the late seventeenth century brought the periodic destruction of property and crops.

The treaty of peace made at Westphalia at the close of the Thirty-years War recognized but three confessions of faith in the German Empire: the Catholic, Lutheran, and Reformed. Whosoever was induced by conscientious conviction to shape his Christian faith differently found his life oppressed by Church and State.

It seems providential that America should open its doors for colonization by these oppressed people who desired to escape the miserable conditions of their war-ravaged land. At the invitation of William Penn, more than 100,000 immigrants had arrived and penetrated the region of the Alleghenies and as far south as Virginia. With all their cultural weakness, these people were at heart religious. Among the immigrants were Johannes and Anna Albrecht who landed in Philadelphia, September 19, 1732, having sailed from Rotterdam on the ship *Johnson* of the Holland-American Line. After taking the oaths of the port denying further allegiance to any foreign power, the Albrechts settled along the Schuylkill River at Fox Mountain, in Douglass Township, near the Montgomery-Berks County Line.

Into this home was born Jacob Albright on May 1, 1757. He was catechized in the Lutheran Church of New Hanover, near Pottstown. As he grew into manhood, on three occasions he served in the Revolutionary War effort. At the age of twenty-six, he married Catherine Cope and moved to a fertile farm in the area of Hahnstown, Lancaster County, two miles southwest of Reamstown. In addition to farming, Albright manufactured tile for roofing. He established a splendid reputation and was known as the "honest tiler." The Albrights united with the Bergstrasse Lutheran Church near Murrell, but later he was dropped from membership because of his evangelical convictions.

Albright was awakened to a spiritual need when illness took the lives of several of his young children in 1790. A Godly, Pietistic Reformed preacher, the Reverend Anthony Houtz, was called to conduct the funeral, and during this preaching Albright was brought under conviction.

Twenty years after the Revolutionary War covered the period of lowest morality in American history. It grieved the heart of Dr. H. M. Muhlenberg, who lamented that the spiritual condition of his people was so miserable that he must shed tears over it. Among the German immigrants were very few clergymen, and this lack of spiritual leaders and pietistic instruction aided the decline of interest in religious matters. Albright lived in a community where evangelical religious experience was frequently stressed. Near his home lived Isaac Davis, a

Methodist who preached the experience of a personal relationship to God. Under this tremendous appeal, Albright yielded to Christ, but the mental anguish suffered under conviction of sin led him through days of much suffering and uncertainty. Gradually he gained courage and strength to express himself in public. Frequently he prayed in the Methodist class meetings and soon was given a written license as an Exhorter, or lay preacher. Before a public address, Albright spent an hour in private prayer and devotion, and it was said that his face literally shone as he preached the Gospel, emphasizing repentance and the conversion experience.

He felt deep sadness because his fellow Pennsylvania Germans knew nothing of the satisfaction that had come to him. When he was absolutely certain that it was not a mere illusion, he finally gave himself to the call of God. In the month of October, 1796, he began his travels in Pennsylvania and Virginia, preaching in homes, barns and schoolhouses, being financially supported by the sale of tile.

He was alone, humanly speaking, when he went forth to preach to his fellow countrymen. He was denied the sympathies of his own family; there was no church or society to cheer him or pray for him. He preached holiness of heart, and purity of life, denouncing use of tobacco and strong drink.

In 1803 Albright met in council with his two assistants, John Walter and Abraham Liesser, and fourteen of his principal laymen at the home of Samuel Liesser in Berks County. This two-day session was the first distinct business session of the followers of Jacob Albright. First of all, they declared themselves an ecclesiastical organization and adopted the Holy Scriptures as their guide and rule of faith. Albright was ordained as a minister of the gospel by his assistants through prayer and laying on of their hands. This was the formal organization of "The Albright People" comprising forty members.

In 1807 the first regular Annual Conference was held at the home of Samuel Becker, near Kleinfeltersville, Lebanon County. Five ministers, three local preachers, and twenty class leaders attended and the conference gave their leader the standing he needed and provided for his ordination. The Conference adopted the episcopal form of government. It is quite obvious that the articles of faith were similar to the Anglican communion and the rituals were like those of the Book of the Common Prayer. The early ministers were not scholastically ignorant for in the preparation of preaching they used the Bible, the Catechism, the Discipline and hymn book which were carried in the saddle bags. Albright continued the practice of fasting and self-discipline even to the last years of his declining health. He had traveled much and far amidst deprivations, cold, heat and strong persecutions of all manner, but he never despaired or faltered.

Albright's health gradually began to fail. In his circuit riding he exposed himself to all kinds of weather, and his physical strength was not equal to the strain. In spite of his weakened condition, he insisted on attending a general meeting at the home of Peter Raidabaugh, Linglestown, nine miles east of Harrisburg. Because of his advanced stage of illness he was unable to preach, but he did manage to sit for a while on the preacher's stand in the barn. Following the meeting, Albright set out toward his home accompanied by friends. When he had covered about thirty miles, he felt that he could not ride all the way to his home. Consequently he directed his horse toward Kleinfeltersville where he was welcomed by the Becker family. Upon his arrival, Albright asked, "Have you my bed ready? I have come to die." During his brief illness, he was in close communion with God, and friends held prayer meetings in his room as he joined his feeble voice in offering praise to God. He retained perfect use of his mental faculties to the last, and insisted he was very grateful that he could die in the presence of Christian people. He bade an affectionate farewell to those present and requested them to unite in praising God. Those who witnessed this were so touched they believed they were near the gates of Heaven. When asked how he felt, he replied, "Happy and heavenly; soon I shall be in Heaven." He died on May 18, 1808, at the age of forty-nine years and seventeen days. He was buried in the Becker family plot on the edge of the village. Near this place, Albright Church was erected in his memory in

Before his death, Albright had preached in twenty-two counties of Pennsylvania and in Maryland and Virginia. Without the leadership of Albright, many felt the work would suffer. His assistant, John Walter, was a powerful preacher but was not gifted with executive ability. George Miller, however, was well-equipped for the task and filled the gap for a period of time until the youthful John Dreisbach, who was only seventeen years of age when he traveled with Albright, and profited greatly by acquiring many of his orderly habits and fine manner of conduct, developed into one of the strong leaders of the new church and served several periods in the legislative halls in Harrisburg.

In 1809, the first Discipline, copied extensively from the Methodist Church, was printed along with the first Catechism book. The center of the church, in a short time, was transferred to the west of the Susquehanna River where her first institutions were established and where she secured her new leaders.

The Ephrata Cloister

JOHN L. KRAFT

TODAY, EPHRATA CLOISTER recalls one of the most unusual experiments in communal living in American history. In Europe, following the Protestant Reformation, unrest developed among the peasant classes, many of whom felt that the reformers had failed to purify the life of the church in conformity to New Testament standards. Out of this general context there evolved the Pietist movement which sought to carry the Reformation further into the area of practical Christian living. Organized were such groups as the Mennonites, Moravians, Dunkards (German Baptist Brethren), and the Inspired which minimized rational doctrine and built upon direct revelation and fellowship. Out of this tradition Ephrata Cloister emerged.

Johann Conrad Beissel, the Cloister founder, as a youth became associated with several Pietist groups and gleaned from them many of the tenets which he later incorporated into his society at Ephrata. As a journeyman baker he traveled through the Rhenish Palatinate absorbing the teachings of the Dunkards and the Inspired, mixing with them the elixir of Rosacrucianism. In 1720 he took advantage of Penn's liberal policy of religious freedom and sailed for the New World, settling in Germantown among the Dunkards. While there he was influenced by Peter Becker, a Dunkard preacher, to establish a new Dunkard congregation in the Conestoga wilderness (Lancaster County). In 1724 he formed the Conestoga congregation, but because of growing doubts concerning the propriety of observing Sunday as the Christian day of rest as opposed to Saturday, the Jewish Sabbath, Beissel in 1728 split with his congregation and moved on into the wilderness to the vicinity of present-day Ephrata. There he established a Sabbatarian community which also advocated celibacy, another practice which Beissel felt was conducive to spiritual growth.

By 1732 enough of his former congregation had followed him that Beissel was obliged to organize his followers into a community of three orders: a celibate brotherhood, a celibate sisterhood, and the married householders. They erected German-style buildings that included dormitories and workhouses for the orders, chapels, mills, shops, and schools. A self-sufficient communal society was built around the celibate orders. Beissel himself, as overseer, prescribed close daily routines filled with work, prayer and meditation. Nightly comforts included a wooden bench with a block of wood for a pillow. Earthly joys were renounced so that the faithful could cultivate the spiritual, and costumes were standardized white garments which virtually covered the body with the exception of the face, hands, and feet.

On approximately two hundred acres of land, the brothers and sisters toiled eighteen hours daily in an attempt to bring God's kingdom to themselves. Each one was assigned his portion of work, which made him self-reliant and disciplined. Sabbath (Saturday) services included preaching, scripture reading and acappella hymn singing. Religious occasions involved communion and feet washing along with the love feast, a meal of Christian fellowship. Nightly midnight meditation lasted for several hours.

In spite of the rigorous schedule which these celibates endured, they demonstrated creative and sensitive natures through art and music. Writing and singing schools cultivated calligraphy and vocal harmony. Some of the most sophisticated fraktur produced by the Pennsylvania Germans was penned by the Cloister members in the 1740's. Included were hand-lettered wall charts, hymnbooks, and book plates. Choirs sang hymns composed by Beissel and some of his followers.

Charity was a vital part of the Cloister way of life. Wayfarers were always welcome. Accommodations included a straw mattress bed and a warm meal given free of charge. Bread was also distributed to the needy of the area. During the Revolution, approximately five hundred wounded soldiers from the Battle of Brandywine were hospitalized under the care of the orders in one of the great buildings. Many who died are buried close by in an adjoining cemetery.

In addition to their operation of several mills, fruit growing, and farming, the brothers were well known for fine printing. Between 1743 and 1830 many important books, pamphlets, deed forms, and broadsides were printed on their press. Included was the largest volume printed in Colonial America, the *Martyrs' Mirror,* a history of the Christian martyrs, which was a favorite book of the German sectarians in Pennsylvania. Papermaking and bookbinding also made the Brotherhood famous.

The Sisterhood devoted much time to domestic occupations including weaving and spinning, the production of sulfur matches, and paper lanterns. Breadbaking for the community was also one of their chief responsibilities.

The success of the society during the mid-eighteenth century centered largely in the person of the founder. Johann Conrad Beissel was a man of charismatic personality and leadership, and his death in 1768 marked the beginning of the end of communal Ephrata. Peter Miller, his successor, carried on the tradition until his death in 1796, but by the end of the eighteenth century the celibate orders had passed on with no one to fill their ranks.

The Brothers' House of the Ephrata Cloister (from an old photograph)

87